The Unbinding

The Unbinding

by WENDY VERGOZ
foreword by Jill Peláez Baumgaertner

RESOURCE *Publications* • Eugene, Oregon

THE UNBINDING

Copyright © 2019 Wendy Vergoz. All rights reserved. Except for brief quotations in critical publications or reviews, no part of this book may be reproduced in any manner without prior written permission from the publisher. Write: Permissions, Wipf and Stock Publishers, 199 W. 8th Ave., Suite 3, Eugene, OR 97401.

Resource Publications
An Imprint of Wipf and Stock Publishers
199 W. 8th Ave., Suite 3
Eugene, OR 97401

www.wipfandstock.com

PAPERBACK ISBN: 978-1-5326-8395-4
HARDCOVER ISBN: 978-1-5326-8396-1
EBOOK ISBN: 978-1-5326-8397-8

Manufactured in the U.S.A.   SEPTEMBER 6, 2019

Excerpts from "Women Don't Riot" from *I Ask the Impossible*. Copyright © 2001 by Ana Castillo.

Psalm 119:94 from *The Book of Common Prayer*. Copyright © 1986 The Church Pension Fund, according to the use of the Episcopal Church.

Scripture quoted from the book of Matthew is from New Revised Standard Version Bible, copyright © 1989 National Council of the Churches of Christ in the United States of America. Used by permission. All rights reserved worldwide.

Scripture quoted from the book of Genesis is from the Holy Bible, NEW INTERNATIONAL VERSION®, NIV® Copyright © 1973, 1978, 1984, 2011 by Biblica, Inc.® Used by permission. All rights reserved worldwide.

Excerpt from "The Fish" from POEMS by Elizabeth Bishop. Copyright © 2011 by The Alice H. Methfessel Trust. Publisher's Note and compilation copyright © 2011 by Farrar, Straus and Giroux. Reprinted by permission of Farrar, Straus and Giroux.

Excerpt from "The Fish" from Poems by Elizabeth Bishop. Published by Chatto & Windus. Reprinted by permission of The Random House Group Limited. © 2011

Italicized portions in Section 5 of "An Evening at the Church Redemption Series" are from "Holy Baptism, Emergency Baptism" in *The Book of Common Prayer*. Copyright © 1986 The Church Pension Fund, according to the use of the Episcopal Church.

Italicized portions in Section 6 of "An Evening at the Church Redemption Series" are from "The Prayers of the People, Form I" in *The Book of Common Prayer*. Copyright © 1986 The Church Pension Fund, according to the use of the Episcopal Church.

Italicized portions of "Ash Wednesday, New Gambier Road" are from "Proper Liturgies for Special Days, Ash Wednesday" in *The Book of Common Prayer*. Copyright © 1986 The Church Pension Fund, according to the use of the Episcopal Church.

For the women who know, and for those who don't but someday will

I am yours; oh, that you would save me!

~ 119:94, *The Book of Common Prayer*, Psalter

A third-millennium call—
from this day on no more, not me, not my daughter,
not her daughter either.

~ Ana Castillo, "Women Don't Riot"

Contents

Foreword by Jill Peláez Baumgaertner | ix
Acknowledgments | xiii

    Turning Over | 1

I. Bully in a Backward Collar

    Sanctuary | 5
    Ask Me | 6
    Bully in a Backward Collar | 7
    The Blueberry Hill Pancake House | 8
    An Evening at the Church Redemption Film Series | 9
    Visitation | 12
    Listen, | 13
    Bitter Vision | 14
    The Cricket Singing at Noon | 15
    Devil's Punch Bowl Canyon | 16
    Ferocious | 17
    Anna's Lament | 19
    April Morning | 20
    Vinalhaven Ferry, Siren Song | 21
    Winter Laces | 22
    The Mother | 23
    The Leonids | 24

II. Take the Bullet

    Village Life | 27
    Funnels Made of Silk | 30
    Cycling | 31
    The Young Church Wife | 32
    Now | 33
    A Geometry of Falling | 34
    Ash Wednesday, New Gambier Road | 36
    The Sound | 37
    Magdalena's Song | 38
    Cuyahoga County, November | 40
    Take the Bullet | 41
    Stuff | 43
    Popsicle | 44
    What's to Happen? | 46
    February | 47

III. 309.81, the Unbinding

    309.81, the Unbinding | 51

IV. Cut the Line and Live

    Pink Impatiens | 65
    Numbers | 66
    Sanctuary 2 | 68
    Filled with Ladders, the World | 69
    No Matter | 72
    A Simple Meal | 74
    St. Helena, California | 75
    Eddie and Donald | 76
    Simple Palms | 77
    Whiplash | 79
    B-Side | 81
    Ghazal to Prey No More | 82
    Asleep, Awake, a Dream | 84
    His First Wife | 89

Foreword

WENDY VERGOZ HAS SURVIVED an extremity of suffering in an abusive marriage to a member of the clergy—a marriage she assumed at the age of twenty-three would be safe because she thought she knew her best friend well—and her response after enduring for over two decades was first to finally leave him, and second to create a poetry of witness. She is one of a long line of poets who have used word and image to reveal trauma, even though many would prefer to mask their suffering. Many are also cowed into silence. Many, in fact, prefer to forget. But Vergoz lays it out for us in all of its harsh and intimate pain. We cannot avoid confronting the evil she has endured. And we cannot avoid asking, as she does, where God was during those years. Not that her life was devoid of beauty of another sort. In "The Mother" she describes the mixture of frustration and irrepressible love that her children invoked:

> I have raised my sweat-wet
> stale-milk-crusted body from the deepest
> sleep . . . Placed by postpartum, stretch-marked self
> in the hands of Prozac. Imagined the clarity
> of uninterrupted thought. Startled at the slightest
> shuffle of blankets in the bassinet.
> And I have grown bitter.
>
> Yet we sway, my son, you in my arms, your
> silken hair against my cheek.

In "The Leonids" she describes a "meteor shower . . . blocked by an overcast sky," yet she recognizes that even if she cannot see them, "still / thousands of particles plunge through space, trailing / their glowing dust," just as her God during these times lurks behind a screen she cannot penetrate.

This realization of the coexistence of two simultaneous but opposite realities permeates her poetry like a miracle.

> What's to happen when the weight
> of air presses like slate,
> yet honey pours like water
> from the children's mouths at night?

God writes straight in crooked lines, the Portuguese say, and this kind of contradiction marks the poet's path. "A silken tangle / of denial and desire, suspicion and faith / disfigurement and beauty, mania and peacefulness. / Is this how God comes to us?" she asks.

The most brilliant, the most demanding, the most resonant poem in this collection of many stunning poems is "309.81, the Unbinding," an expert weaving of the story of the binding of Isaac with the poet's own growing awareness that she was, like Isaac, blindly complicit in her own binding—in her case, within a disastrous marriage. "309.81" refers to the entry in the *Diagnostic and Statistical Manual of Mental Disorders* that describes PTSD.

> Isaac, did you know?
> Did you use your voice?
> Did you have a voice?
> But you, yourself, carried the wood.
> *And I, myself, carried the fire and the knife.*
> *Blind, myself, I carried the fire and the knife.*
> Once blind. Now aware.
> Tears don't come. Tears won't come.
> Awareness is a curse, a different
> kind of binding.

The steak knife, thrown at her by her abuser, was a wedding present. And now, many years later "I left and I *am* left. / Left bound, unbound, unbinding."

> Even here. Even this place binds me,
> for it bound me years ago with lies.

Foreword

The seminary binds
And the ram
Chapels bind
And wood
Stained glass binds
And fire
For both of us, the knife.

Bound to "Lift High the Cross" to coffee hour
to choir trips and sermons.
Bound to lie. Bound to smile.
To smile no matter what, no matter
knife or phone or keys
Wood or fire or knife.

And then she asks, "*Where was Sarah? Where was I? . . . Where was God?*" God was in her resolve to leave and to not return to her abuser. God was in the journey she travels from "I can't leave him . . . We have too much stuff" to realizing, "Enough. The End. Never more." God was in the acknowledgment that the sweetness of the gelato she spoons into her mouth was "simply not enough." And God is in the poet's truth-telling and both the tender and the raw reckonings of her poetic lines. Even though the poetic style is quite different, I am reminded of Gerard Manley Hopkins's "Terrible Sonnets," filled with angst and doubt and the torture of God's silence. Wendy Vergoz rehearses these themes, which are as old as poetry itself, but she asks the questions in a new context, startling, disturbing, anchored in the fallen world but simultaneously reaching toward a particularly elusive *deus absconditus*.

—Jill Peláez Baumgaertner
   Professor of English Emerita
   Wheaton College

Acknowledgments

Grateful acknowledgment is made to the following magazines or exhibitions in which these poems have appeared, some in slightly different versions:

Anglican Theological Review: "Ash Wednesday, New Gambier Road," "Cuyahoga County, November," "Pink Impatiens," and "The Leonids."

Arts Kaleidoscope: Art, Poems & Video, Gallery 308, Muncie, Indiana: "No Matter."

The Christian Century: "Visitation," "Now," "Vinalhaven Ferry, Siren Song," "Listen," and "Funnels Made of Silk."

Cleaver Magazine: "Eddie and Donald."

Dystrumpian Almanac: "Whiplash" and "Ghazal to Prey No More."

50/50: Poems & Translations by Women over 50: "His First Wife" and "Popsicle." Quills Edge Press.

Flying Island: "Anna's Lament," "Filled with Ladders, the World," and "The Blueberry Hill Pancake House."

Ground: "What's to Happen," "An Evening at the Church Redemption Film Series," and "Magdalena's Song."

Dreams & Sacrifices: Stories of Genesis Reimagined, Arthur M. Glick JCC, Indianapolis, Indiana: "Filled with Ladders, the World."

ACKNOWLEDGMENTS

Literary Mama: "A Geometry of Falling."

Mothers Always Write: "The Sound."

Panoply: "Bitter Vision."

Pink Panther Magazine: "Bully in a Backward Collar," "Sanctuary," "Sanctuary 2," and "Stuff."

Reimagine, an RSA Retrospective, The Harrison Center, Indianapolis, Indiana: "Filled with Ladders, the World."

Religion, Spirituality, and the Arts, hosted by Butler University, Indianapolis, Indiana, funded by Lilly Endowment Inc., CICF in partnership with Christian Theological Seminary: "309.81, the Unbinding."

Spirit & Place: Living the Dream, Indianapolis Artsgarden: "Asleep, Awake, A Dream."

"Winter Laces," Honorable Mention in the Non-rhyming Poetry category of the 85th Annual *Writer's Digest* Writing Competition.

Special thanks to the Arts Council of Indianapolis and the Indiana Arts Commission whose funding contributed to the creation of this book, to The Napa Valley Writers Conference where a number of these poems found their beginnings, and to Religion, Spirituality, and the Arts which played a significant role in the genesis of the book's final incarnation.

With deep gratitude to the following people who have been important influences in my life, writing and otherwise: Jill Peláez Baumgaertner, Erin Belieu, James Kimbrell, Jeremy Countryman, Claire Messud, John Kinsella, Jane Hirshfield, Elizabeth Alexander, Laura Storrs, Norbert Krapf, Sofia Starnes, and Rohan Preston. Liz Forman and Laura Darling. Steve Replogle, Steve Kascht, and Whitney Cobb. Kate Wiley and Renée Ruderman. Barb Shoup. Sandy Eisenberg Sasso. Julie Eflin and Sofiya Inger. JL Kato, Terry Ofner, and Kyle Craig. Dave Shumate and George LaMaster. Liza Hyatt and Jim Powell. Mike Orfe and Kim Helsel. Cathleen Case, Lynn Salit, Erin Lyons, Steve Morris, Susan Benjamin, Judi Elman, and especially

Acknowledgments

Jean Nussbaum. Carolyn Jurkowitz, Billie Shire, and Angela Hunnicutt. Kathy Thomson. Lee and Deb. Neil and John. Heather and Cheryl, Jen and Allison. Abby, Joey, Hannah, and Lori. My students over the years, especially Clarissa. Susan Weitzman and the Weitzman Center. Prevail, Inc. Elease Womack and the amazing women in the UBC Writing Workshop. My interns. Marcia and Carla, Diane and Martine. Jamey. Lindy. Alice. Ned and Bev. Theodora. Joanna. Carol. Jack, Robin, Mom and Dad. N and L.

Turning Over

"More tick-en!" my son cries
from his highchair as I cut
the supermarket bird
with a steak knife, a wedding gift.

At midnight I wake: husband lying
next to me, son asleep
across the hall, daughter
in her bassinet.

The ceiling fan whirs above
slashing the air like a scythe.
Turn to sleep *steak knife*.
Turn again *wedding gift*.

Steak knife, wedding gift.
Pull the sheet around me, white.

I

Bully in a Backward Collar

Sanctuary

I said "Yes" when he asked. Chose him
to be safe. Best friend meant no plunge,
everything predictable, I thought.

He preaches from the pulpit. I sit silent
in a pew. His silver-tongued *peace
and truth, mercy and justice* engulf me.

Cathedral. Incense surrounds me.
Husband processes past. Bruises
on my arms unseen beneath my sweater.

The granite font holds water.
His hands throw a knife.
Another day baptize our child.

Raise the chalice. Break bread.
Download pornography: *Tie me up
so you can do whatever you want to me.*

Tenth anniversary wine.
His serpent tongue drowns me:
You like it so much have more.

Ask Me

and I'll tell you
of unfinished business,
the horror of first love.
Not love. No.

Ask me, a survivor, a one-in-six statistic,
and I'll tell you of an evil calculation.
Vodka clear as water, clear as darkness
through that window, clear as light.

Ask me and I'll tell you of an eighteen-year-old
devil—an angel-seeming devil—
his name hidden twenty-seven years,
penciled on a desk drawer,
today I scratch it off.
Twenty-seven years ago, I,
a fifteen-year-old girl,
lay corpse-like on the carpet
near that desk.

Ask me, I might tell you
now my daughter has that desk.

Ask me and I'll tell you of the vodka
clear as truth, clear as darkness
past the window, clear as lies.
A one-in-six statistic, corpse-like
on blue carpet, bitter liquid in her veins.

Looking back through vodka
to a window clear with darkness,
ask me, I will tell you
of no consolation, no conversation,
till now.

Bully in a Backward Collar

outward bliss
domestic hiss

public creed
domestic greed

prominent sage
domestic rage

communion chalice
domestic malice

pastor yet
domestic threat

palpable silence
domestic

The Blueberry Hill Pancake House

parking lot
on the East side
of town
is where
I picked up
my laptop
from the forensic
specialist,
plus the flash drive
of Lydea and
her girlfriends,
the pornographic
clips
my husband
the pastor
had downloaded
onto my computer
six days before
he sent the letter
to his congregation
promising
with confidence
that there is
nothing
scandalous
about
our divorce.

An Evening at the Church Redemption Film Series

> *"Weren't you happy when the guard beat that rapist, crippled him?"*
>
> ~ comment at a church dinner after watching *The Shawshank Redemption*

1. Genesis

Perhaps it begins
with a kernel
of dung, broken bits of

2. The Morning After

Bile I tasted when I recollected
the pieces
of now-thawed conversation.
The night before
I'd swallowed their solid
forms with swig after
swig of wine.

3. Grace and the Meal (Luke 6:27–38)

Love the filo dough,
embrace the salad greens,
do not withhold the spinach pie,
give to everyone pinot noir,
do not condemn, forgive,
aren't we all just *be merciful*
wonderful?

4. Breaking Bread

I wouldn't walk there, he
said at the table, words
shred air into
splinters, pierce
ear eye lung palm
with darkness nailed
through
not in that neighborhood.

5. Emergency Baptism

In case of emergency, any
baptized person
may administer red wine, I
drank another glass
and tried to sift through
piles of words swirling
on the table top.

6. The Prayers of the People

"We were driving along"
For the poor and oppressed
"when he stopped the cab"
For the unemployed and the destitute
"at the red light and said,"
For prisoners and captives
"'on that corner you'd be dead.'"

7. Re: deem

Regret, rewind, resist, refute, redirect, remake, refuse
remind, reconstruct, remorse, revile, revenge
reproach, reform
recreate, revoice, rework, rewrite,
re: righteousness, re: self
rebuke

Visitation

Adams Street. 5 p.m.
I exit Union Station.
Horn blasts punctuate
urban roar, heat waves
swell from asphalt.
Closed faces shoot past,
wingtips whisk them by.
Seven months pregnant,
I plod on cracked concrete,
struggling to dodge
the raven-suited flow.
Someone elbows me.
My arms circle my child.
Sweat running down my neck,
my hair sticking together
in wet strands,

I drop into a taxi.
The driver stares ahead,
but the mirror betrays
the tumid cauliflower
of his face, his neck,
his scalp. I swallow hard,
"Art Institute, please."
A boy smiles at me
from a Polaroid taped
to the dashboard.
The child within me leaps.
Stuck to tattered vinyl,
I sink into the seat and shut
my eyes. His cab labors
against the traffic's
jarring, turbulent tide.

Listen,

There is nothing new here.
Rain falls on closed peonies.
There is nothing new.
Yesterday my son brought me honeysuckle
from the garden.
Today his hair smells of citrus.

But that's all,
nothing more,
not so much as a grain of salt on the tongue,
only rain falling on peonies
that are closed.

Bitter Vision

Standing at the mirror, my son's harsh
whine piercing, my daughter's sharp wail jarring,
I brush my hair, silken, smooth.

I will myself: remember the downy circle
of crown first seen.
But gaping flesh births not just child.
The twisting, blue-black cord
wraps around my neck.
Neck snapped, still do brick-red nipples
offer—marble-cold, my body yields
warm milk.

The Cricket Singing at Noon

The clamor of silverware falling
into a wooden drawer, of finding
her firstborn's dress molding in the cellar.
I baptize the children's feet
in the creek, water flowing like vodka.
As noiselessly as painting
with horsehair brushes,
the stone foundation flakes away.

Blossoms scorn the dogwood.
The bishop eats on paper plates
and drinks just ginger ale.
I read then shred a letter: my father's
losing vision, turmoil on the retina.
The clamor of raindrops
striking the parsonage roof,
of finding the speckled eggs gone.

Devil's Punch Bowl Canyon

Crested Butte,
Colorado.
10,722 feet.
Schofield Pass.
State's most
deadly.
Vehicle Traffic
Discouraged.
He drives.
Kids in back.
Me in front.
Round a bend.
Neon sign:
Last chance
to turn around!
Rock ledge road.
Cliff-edge cut.
One lane.
No guardrail.
Steep ravine—
300-foot drop.
Grip the seat.
One car
squeezes past.
Tow-truck
coming at us.
Kids hold
their breath.
I hold my
breath.
He laughs.

Ferocious

Like a dog
licking a carcass,
the only food
he'd had in days,
he licked me
ferociously
I splay-legged
on a bamboo bed
all but passed out
licked me
ferociously
as if I might
wake up
and tell him
no.

Wine poured
into me
poured into me
repeatedly
poured in as if he knew
this might be
his only chance:
tenth-anniversary
you-like-it-so-much-
have-more
celebration
poured in
ferociously
as if he knew.

*A dog
licking a carcass
me splay-legged
passed out
his only chance
wine is poured
and husband licks
wine is poured
and husband licks
wine is poured
and me splay-legged
while husband licks
I might wake up
and interrupt
his dog-like tongue.*

Thirteen years since
*wine was poured
and husband's tongue
corkscrew switchblade
dagger tongue
slaying me
consuming me
a carcass
on a bamboo bed.*

Anna's Lament

> *And all at once a strange idea came to her:*
> *what if he had ceased to love her?*
> ~ Leo Tolstoy, Anna Karenina

To swim under iron and count,
each day, the ways I am alone.

No matter his touch, or not,
no matter silence to my words.

My nature, coreopsis,
coreopsis in a world of stone.

Too soon depleted, I choke on
dried petals, drink morphine.

Who knows such wounds,
ignominy and a lost son?

Wooden ties taunt, "What for?"
and promise something new.

I drop the red bag, drown my
sullied body in an iron sea.

April Morning

Thursday to the skin doctor, barnacle
removed. Old, he said, that doctor
    of the barnacle.

My friend in a middle-age crisis bought
a Volvo as a cure. A red herring, I say,
    as I drive Route 36.

Five dead deer tied to a flatbed trailer.
A large feral cat, bloated molasses.

The radio claims that rats gnawed
corpses at an L.A. garage, but
    I don't believe it.

Limbs downed by the ice storm, split now
into logs. Red-snouted, a dog lifts his head
    from the carcass of a deer.

Vinalhaven Ferry, Siren Song

Disarming, really, this surging night-dark water.
A harbor seal slips, oil-black, into the sea's
engulfing folds. On the ferry, three girls eat cherries,

slurp ruby juice from fruit, palm, and finger,
linger over pulp. Those black, sea-skimming
cormorants dive into Atlantic waves,

then rise with hooked beaks full.
Three girls consume that succulent fruit,
spit brown pits into crimson hands, pluck plump

cherries from a red-soaked plastic bag.
Their mother leans upon a rail, enthralled
by thoughts of a crustacean mob at work

beneath the shuddering sea. The ferry sways
on night-dark swells, heaves toward
nuns and cans. Bare legs dangling

and rose-wet hair tangling, three girls ripen
hands in flesh, drizzle chins with wine.
A hidden ledge, a granite coast, a fierce,

a laughing tide. Beguiled by forgotten currents,
you cannot not imbibe—three girls, mouths
dripping cherry juice, foreheads scarlet-streaked,

tap feet and pluck again.
Beauty no excuse.

Winter Laces

Our ten-year-old knees in snow drifts.
    Ice skates over a shoulder,
one in front and one behind,
    their promise taps against me.

Elizabeth's slender body bends over skates,
    hands plaiting laces on metal hooks
then wrapping them, lace by lace,
    around the leather tops.

We skate on the pond through the deepness
    of powder, the scrape of two shovels,
till we need clear no more.
    Then no words

    just metal cutting curves,
        our skates weaving through drifts,
    binding the seams of ice
        together glide by glide.

Brightness of snow, darkness of ice,
    pattern of paths, black winter lace.
The white passion, the drowsy splendor
    when nothing mars the stillness

    of one white December morning.

The Mother

O god, I do not have it in me
to change the diapers filled with mustard-smears
of shit, or wipe the sour chunks of oatmeal
from their chins. I have raised my sweat-wet
stale-milk-crusted body from the deepest
sleep, I have scrubbed acrid vomit
from my hair and clothes, I have held the thrashing
limbs of a fiery two-year-old, his sister's voice howling
from upstairs, every hair on my body wanting
solitude. Placed my postpartum, stretch-marked self
in the hands of Prozac. Imagined the clarity
of uninterrupted thought. Startled at the slightest
shuffle of blankets in the bassinet.
And I have grown bitter.

Yet we sway, my son, you in my arms, your
silken hair against my cheek.

The Leonids

Bird shadows pass on clapboard like storms, on sidewalk
and street like storms. They say a man dropped
out of a plane, 9,000 feet to Texas.
Small flames in the orchard, yellow leaves on
McIntosh limbs defy November's decree.
At night a 10:50 phone call and my mind imagines
the worst. Brook water murmurs through
windowpanes: *living full of death, living faced
with life*. Tonight the Leonid meteor shower
is blocked by an overcast sky, still
thousands of particles plunge through space, trailing
their glowing dust.

II

Take the Bullet

Village Life

1. Bats

Bats are in the house.
The first flies through
the living room.

The next is in our son's
closet, hangs between toddler
shirts and sweaters.
I slide the closet door sideways,
see the tiny, dark body
upside down with wings
closed but ready for flight.

2. Walls

In our library, bookshelves line
one wall. A nineteenth-century stone
fireplace takes up another.
The piano he plays sits on the third.
The fourth wall, between library
and living room, has French doors
painted gold and a hole
he punched
through the forest green wall.
Frayed wallboard, a gray-edged gap
in forest green paint, broadcasts
his fist for months.

Frayed wallboard twelve years before.
A month after we got married
he punched
a hole in our kitchen wall,
a gray-edged ring

bounded by white paint
just below the stairs leading
to the bedrooms in the widow's
house we rented.

3. Sandbox

Backyard sandbox. Babbling
stream. Wooden bridge. Our son
pushes his bubble mower
over the never-ending grass.
Grass and grass, so much
grass that he insists that the parish
employ someone to cut it.

He creates a terraced garden
out front. A picture window
offers a view from street
to living room.
He says people look
through our recycling.

4. ER

Midnight rage. His screams
wake our daughter whose frightened
sobs trigger her asthma.
He leaves. I call a friend to stay
with our son, asleep
on the other side of the house,
take our daughter to the ER.

5. Silence

A violent silence. He moves
into the guest room.

6. Assistant Rector

His assistant accuses him of abuse:
> *Volcanic eruptions*
> *Threatened explosions*
> *Isolation, Domination*
> *Impossible to work for him*
> *and remain sane and sound.*

He lies to the bishop.
Forces her to resign
> *She serves at my pleasure.*

Tells me he'll make sure that
she never works in a church again.

7. Payphone

I leave. Drive halfway to Michigan
where my parents live. Stop
at a payphone. Call my parents,
sobbing, say I left but
have to turn around, can't leave
the kids, don't want them
to grow up in a broken home.

Drive back to them, to him.

Meanwhile he calls my parents
> *She's unstable*

tells parishioners
that he wouldn't leave me
alone with our kids.
> *It's not safe for them.*

Funnels Made of Silk

It's fall and the grass spiders, the funnel weavers,
have entered the house.
Last year the shower of Leonids,
now, daughter, you in my arms.

Yesterday, after last rites, my husband helped
find a casket for a three-year-old.
Today he took communion
to a boy in the hospital.
The body and blood now sit in a box
on our kitchen counter.

After the nebulizer has freed the chambers
of your lungs, I carry you to your room.
Another yellow snail has died in your aquarium.
My fingers cradle its lightness,
toss it in the garbage.

Once in bed, you sleep the sleep of danger,
breath clicking upon itself.
Get behind me! I whisper you to say.

The grass spider wants dark corners,
even with four sets of eyes.
Between the bricks and doorframe waits
a funnel made of silk.

Cycling

1. Bike Path Near Zion Road

November and a corridor
    of glowing, golden trees.
"Nothing wrong with our Rector that a whack
    with a 2x4 wouldn't fix."
Copperhead snake, Stull Road,
    soybeans in the wind.
What to make of the afternoon sun
    warming the asphalt below?
Emptied of sweet clover, Killduff's field
    makes room for early frost.

2. Bike Path, Kokosing River

At 5:21 the first bird sings, the stream
    that runs to anywhere.
Blue heron, bluebird, kingfisher, dragonfly.
    A village full of loneliness.
What to do with, rotting in the water's flow,
    the carcass of a fawn.
After Howard Station, a pale yellow butterfly
    teeters on the wind.

The Young Church Wife

After William Carlos Williams's
"The Young Housewife"

At thirty-eight, the pastor's wife
moves behind the hollow
walls of the parsonage.
Parishioners pass by, peer
through a picture window:

    Then again she scoops oatmeal
    into the baby's bowl, spoons sugar
    into her husband's mug,
    then again opens the paper
    at his chair, searches
    the fridge, kisses the baby.

Then again he appears: prayer book poised,
collar sharp, wingtips harsh
upon parquet.

Now

What might be left
has vanished.
Paradise trees, spindle leaves
once green, berries ruby-red.
Now dry magenta tentacles
and fruit withered, black.
The god of gaps.

What might be left
has vanished:
dew as thick as raindrops,
doe's hooves striking
solid ground, spider bowls
in fresh-cut wheat,
now gone.

Distant voices mumble.
The wind slams shut
a wooden door,
the tattered sky
looms, ashen.
Spinners gild
a dust-bound earth.

A Geometry of Falling

Felix Culpa, O Happy Fall

1

Think of a woman
vacuuming her stairway rug

beneath a window's
angled stare,

pausing only
to notice

in rhombic light,
a diamond fractal of carpet

or to lose herself
in frenzied sound,

till she sees she's on
a spondee and words

ping-pong in her brain.

2

Some say pomegranate but I say
apple, Eve's tempter,

now thurifer of Autumn air.
The wind coaxes

Cortland branches to drop
their cider-bound load.

Shadows toss their lanky limbs
upon the vesper earth.

Barn swallows skim the ground
and rise again, skim and rise,

the rapid gradient
of their flight

almost a stumble.

3

A Tuesday morning.
I'm at the kitchen sink when

my son walks in.
For you, he says as

a stone spills
from his fingers, descends

like a tangent
to land

heart-shaped *(yes)*
against my soap-wet palm.

We trip from grace
to grace,

O Happy Fall.

Ash Wednesday, New Gambier Road

you hate nothing you have made

the robin bleeds on asphalt
dust, rasping notes, hymn
failing, whisper

remember that you are

the monarch skips off the Ford,
black-edged wings blaze
to the ground, heavy as slate

you shall return to

a dead crow flutters in traffic,
pearl-black wings throw back
the sun, plummet to the earth

The Sound

of my daughter falling
out of bed was really
the sound of a stolen car
hitting a tree in front
of the neighbor's house.
The thieves,
two teenage boys,
soundlessly jump
the wrought-iron gate
to our front yard,
run down the path beside
our house then jump again,
the backyard fence,
throwing wild footprints
in the blossoming,
still-falling snow.

Magdalena's Song

> *"Look at the birds of the air: they neither sow nor reap*
> *nor gather into barns, and yet your heavenly Father feeds them.*
> *Are you not of more value than they?"*
> ~ Matthew 6:26 (NRSV)

1

Magdalena's fingers bustle, knitting
short-armed sweaters near

a storefront on Division Street.
WHORE, she barks through yellow teeth at women

who pass by. Her plastic Jesus watches them
wear high-heels every day.

At night the bat's glide lulls her
and her downcast eyelids sweep through time

like sparrow's wings.

2

The sparrow's nest is softest,
made of horsehair, not of twigs.

Spilling from the hayloft, cobwebs tulle
the dust-bound earth below.

Thin red claws notch skyward,
eight chickens dangle from a clothesline

*(the most efficient way to kill them). Maggie's hands,
her smooth girl hands, nudge under hens for eggs,*

silken, oval, warm.

3

Magdalena warms her hands
in a half-full bag of popcorn,

nods to Jesus.
High-heels tick past, car horns screech,

the laughter of a passing child
distracts her from her echoed curse.

Hanging from her tattered sleeves,
Maggie's hands *her smooth girl hands* caress

a fragment of cement.

Cuyahoga County, November

Lingering leaf of autumn
flows into a grate, becomes
paint, becomes wine, becomes blood.
Poison floods a heart made numb

by vacant, negligent touch.
Indian summer's enough
warmth to thaw skin, but not bone.
Eclipsed and unknown heart, rough

hewn by early frost. At home
the children sleep. A somber tone
washes their milky slumber.
Iced heart, the crumbler, alone,

of dreams. Cold unencumbered
disrupts the lives that once were
fragrant in their dawn. Late
God, my heart is now humbler

than Autumn's last liberated
leaf. This heart, isolated,
joins the leaf and disappears,
blood clearing down an iron grate.

Take the Bullet

At least you didn't get knocked up,
my husband says when
I tell him I was raped at fifteen.

Later he tells a story to inspire me:
A man who was shot
went on a speaking tour
to tell others how glad he was
that he'd been shot.
He wouldn't be who he is
without it,
so he wears the bullet
on a chain around his neck.
Sometimes you just have to take
the bullet, he says.

Just take the bullet.
Lie back on the medium blue
carpet, let the bullet
come again.
You wouldn't be
who you are
without the bullet,
so take the bullet, he says.
He dangled the bullet
and explained that things
happen for a reason,
that if he had to do it
over again, he would.
So I take the bullet.
Again and again

the bullet pounds into me
again and again
lie back on the medium blue
medium blue carpet
just go back and
take the bullet.
Things happen
for a reason.
Take
the bullet.

Stuff

SafeRacks Overhead Garage Storage Combo Kit.
Two 4-x-8-foot ceiling racks stuffed
with coolers, camping equipment, ski boots,
kid's clothes, Lincoln Logs, Tinker Toys.
Boxes of photos, grad school papers,
suitcases, my wedding dress—confident
our daughter would wear it one day—boxed
by professional dry cleaners then encased
in a muslin drawstring bag to preserve it
for years to come.

I sit in the driver's seat, car parked
under the SafeRacks in our tiny garage,
a two-story ladder bungee-corded
to the wall beside me, barely enough
room to get out.

I gaze in front of me: wall shelves.
Five rows of wall shelves filled
with basketballs, soccer balls, Frisbees,
roller blades, hiking poles, bicycle
pumps, helmets. Tennis balls,
toilet paper, paper towels, laundry soap.
Garbage bags, Lawn & Leafs.
Extra towels, old sheets.
Sterilite bins jammed with Christmas
ornaments, wrapping paper, ribbon.
Sterilite bins stuffed with Halloween decorations,
plastic orange and black pumpkins, a fake
glow-in-the-dark headstone on a shelf nearby.
I can't leave him, I think. *We have too much
stuff. We could never untangle.*

Popsicle

It's a Popsicle,
he said
think that it's a Popsicle.
I said,
"I don't like it."
But he said
What about what I like?
Popsicle.
Lazy August evening.
Michigan.
Five years old.
Not this.

Popsicle, he said.
I said, "No."
And he said
Just for a bit
knowing
that I hated it.

Popsicle.
Julie and me
on banana-seat bikes
zipping home
through fireflies
for popsicles.
Not this.
Not this popsicle.

When I read
of the Sofitel
housekeeper
in New York,
I think about
Popsicle, think that
I think about

the screened-in-porch
in Michigan,
five years old
I hold a melting
popsicle
think that it's a
fireflies blinking
in August's hot air
Popsicle.
Think that.
Just for a bit.

What's to Happen?

> *"Are not two sparrows sold for a penny?*
> *Yet not one of them will fall to the ground apart from your Father."*
> ~ Matthew 10:29 (NRSV)

What's to happen when the weight
of air presses like slate,
yet honey pours like water
from the children's mouths at night?

I sit in sunlight at my father's desk,
take out each drawer, pressed
for answers. The small one yields
just dust. As a girl I confessed

my sins each week, but now I maintain
a desert's silence. The dust contains
a voice, *a sparrow falls*, misplaced
so long it's now a grieved refrain.

When I lift my son's light frame,
I whisper in his ear, *for shame,*
I am alone. He stirs and breathes
and the scent of honey claims

my lost attention. I turn
toward—I lay down the boy, return
to the desk in hope of discerning,
then fold myself into its polished wood.

February

Five shades of gray, the sky
would yield to scissors' edge, reveal
a flare beyond its haze, a blackberry
sun. I drive past twelve solitary
barns, a sullen sky watches
me, catches me in sunlight or
in rain. Reins in hand an Amish
farmer guides his plow pulled by
square-legged horses dark
as eggplant. Girls in moonlight smoke
cigarettes, send circles toward the sun
through—a flight of sparrows
hovers, Angus cows roam muddy
hills, hay bales float through stubbled
fields. It was all I could do not
to drive into a passing truck, passes
me on the two-lane road, I on my way
to anywhere but—I couldn't not
go, couldn't just turn and go or slow
and stop. The asphalt scroll says
stop, I go, I melt into the cornfield's
frost, into my child's next—February's
stark sky catches me and won't
relent. A stray calf drifts past rusty
wheels, artificial flowers skim
grassy graves. I gaze toward girls
who glide down gravel paths
in my daughter's favorite—daughter's
face shaped like sun or moon
which catches me, pulls me back
as I head into traffic, oncoming
two-lane-undivided-highway-truck-

traffic full of blackberries
hay bales or cigarettes, pulls
me back before, it's raining, but
not too late.

III

309.81, the Unbinding

309.81, the Unbinding

309.81 is the code for PTSD in the 4th edition of the Diagnostic and Statistical Manual of Mental Disorders.

Wounds that can't be seen are more painful than those that can be seen and cured by a doctor.
~ Nelson Mandela

Abraham took the wood for the burnt offering and placed it on his son Isaac, and he himself carried the fire and the knife.
~ Genesis 22:6 (NIV)

1

Isaac, did you know?
Were you shell-shocked?
Knife-shocked?
Perhaps you
Thought
Such violence normal.
Don't.

2

The altar, the wood, the fire, the knife.
The knife, the keys, the phone, the wall.
A testing of faith?
Priests wield knives, throw knives,
throw keys, throw phones, punch walls.
I wither.

3

Isaac, did you know?
Did you use your voice?
Did you have a voice?
But you, yourself, carried the wood.
And I, myself, carried the fire and the knife.
Blind, myself, I carried the fire and the knife.
Once blind. Now aware.
Tears don't come. Tears won't come.
Awareness is a curse, a different
kind of binding.

4

Steak knife, wedding gift.
That day, bound for binding.
Thirty years later
DSM-4 diagnosis 309.81.
Still sometimes bound.
Lost myself for twenty-two years.
PTS
Disorder. Destruction. Despair.
Sorrow.
A gaping wound.
Isaac, does it end? Sarah, did it end?
And yet I left.
I left and I *am* left.
Left bound, unbound, unbinding.

5

Isaac, I see you in the paintings,
Rembrandt—your father's hand clamps your face
    your smooth, youthful neck exposed

Caravaggio—your father grips your neck, your cheek, your jaw
    your young face terrified
del Sarto—ready to kill, Abraham towers over
    your slender-boy body, hands bound, eyes wide, confused
Pittoni—you are blindfolded and your hands work a blue cloth
    (were you plotting an escape?)
Isaac, does the blindfold soften the blow?

6

The knife brandished by your father,
unpointed blade, perfectly sharp, perfectly smooth,
not serrated. Finely honed and free
from the slightest notch.
One and a half to two times as long as your neck was wide.

The knife thrown by my husband,
Regent Sheffield Stainless Steel.
Steak knife. One in a set of six.
Four-and-a-half-inch pointed blade
I should have called the police

Hard, black plastic handle.
Blade's serrated edge
guaranteed forever sharp
Black and white his clericals.
Sawtooth-sharp that knife
I still can see it coming

7

Isaac, did you see it coming?

Abraham took the knife to slay his son.
"I will make your descendants *took the knife*

as numerous as the stars in the *to slay his son* sky
it will be their inheritance forever."
Abraham took the knife to slay his
son guaranteed forever bound.

Guaranteed bound.
One month married,
a first punch through wallboard.
More would follow
Isaac, your wrists bound by cords
Mine bruised by hands.

Did Sarah pull the knife out? Or Ishmael?
I pulled my knife out. No one else.
Just me.
It took me twenty-two years to see
No one told me it was there (!?)
But I pulled it out.

Wedding gift.
Regent Sheffield stainless
stained
I gave those knives away. The set.
But buried one in a drawer
to remind me of what I left
and what I deserve.

8

Sorting and sifting.
I threw out even the garbage can.
Bound to can to knife to car to thought,
every thought a prison,
a strap, a rope, a cord.
Prisoner to can to knife to car to socks,

black knee socks—*I cannot stand.*
Prisoner to knife to car to socks,
that specific car, blue Prius.
Every fucking blue Prius reminds me
I was bound.
Bound no more.

9

Even here. Even this place binds me,
for it bound me years ago with lies.

The seminary binds
And the ram
Chapels bind
And wood
Stained glass binds
And fire
For both of us, the knife.

Bound to "Lift High the Cross" to coffee hour
to choir trips and sermons.
Bound to lie. Bound to smile.
To smile no matter what, no matter
knife or phone or keys
Wood or fire or knife

Steps and a voice
No voice
Throat cut throat closed
Bound
Where was Sarah? Where was I?

Where was God?

Bound by no protective order.
Bound by no collar.
Bound by no vows, no sacrament.
Nothing sacred, nothing holy, nothing clean.
All tainted, poisoned, touched by venom:
Prius and men in clericals,
priests in—*notice*—backwards collars.

Bound by the jewelry box he ransacked
The gold necklaces he measured
The bank account he cleaned out
The bruises on my arms
Bound even by the garbage can
Even the fucking garbage can

You don't need me to tell you. You know it, Sarah.
Knife in me and knife in son. Sarah pulled it out.

Bound by his philosophy: "To make a woman comply,
break her down until she cries—she's putty in your hands."
She is bound.

Bound by silence.
Bound by threats.

Even here even now bound by stained glass scraps
and empty halls. The lies
of an imposter therapy session.

Freed!
Bound no more.
I throw it out. Even the garbage can.

10

Wood, fire, knife, ram
Anything tainted goes

Garage Sale Exorcism. My people help with it:
John, Carla, Mackenzie, Alice.
Angela, Demi, Danielle.
Isaac, who helps you? Sarah and Hagar? Ishmael?
309.81—*can trauma go for sale?*

They don't understand the need to shed.
Understand the need to shed.
Understand the haunting.
PTSD
Prius
Trash can
Socks
Disorder

The glasses must go. Clarity. No cloudy glass.
The recipe box. Clean out the recipe box.
CDs must go. Ella F. and Louis.
Cash, Peyroux, and Elvis.
Even the favorites *tainted* gone.
Seven times I scrubbed the slate
polished it on my knees.

Pinot Noir, gone.
Blue umbrella, gone.
Gold necklace, gone.
Candlesticks, gone.
Jewelry box, gone.
Desk, gone.
Bed, gone.

Kitchen table, gone.
Mirrors, rugs, mixer, gone.
Old rug, imposter rug, you're not what
I thought you were
sold a bill of goods
You're gone.
Where I stand?
Not on that rug. Not in that car.

Even the in-between must go.
Towels and sheets, picture frames,
artwork, plants, and tools.
Even the house must go.

The new knives are not as sharp.
Welcome, knives, welcome.

11

Isaac, I see you in the paintings.
Eyes covered, throat gripped.
Can't breathe. No voice.
Your tender body, skinny-boy body, slender, hairless
Sarah's son.

My husband's name is father.
My husband's name was father.
No father, no farther. No more.

I cannot hear the music. Still bound
so cannot hear the *Lift High* the music.
Sick. Ill. Trauma. Post.
If post, why present?

Still bound. Not bound. Unbinding. Untying the truth.

Steak knife, wedding gift, wedding ring, gone.
The birds will come: yellow finch, sparrow,
cardinal, and chickadee.
I feed them each morning.

12

Tie the knot
Steak knife wedding
Untie the knot
Not who I thought he was
Blessed be the ties that
Blessed be the ties that bind?
Not this tie. Not this knot.
God doesn't bind like this.

What God has bound together
God help her, help her tear it asunder,
help her unbind God didn't bind,
wouldn't want, this.

Isaac, remember, God doesn't bind like
Where was God?

13

Bound by husband
Bound by father
Bound by fear, by shame, by silence
You carried the wood and the shame
Line cut
Throat ungripped
Voice now unbound.

The dogwood will be planted, will blossom.
The wind chimes are ringing, even in December.
I hear cars in the distance. They aren't coming for me.
No, Isaac, not for me and not for you.

14

Isaac, you and I are bound by
our inheritance forever
wounds unseen and unforeseen
domestic: a father, a husband
violence: thousands of years apart
shellshock
it is our inheritance
309.81
forever

wholly bound by
a most unholy sacrifice

15

Isaac, what did you shed?
Get out of the car. Never again. No.
Even the garbage can will go.

Shoes. Socks. Desert. Dust. Sun. Son. Ram.

Even the in-between must go.
Nothing holy. Few things whole.
What is sacred? All is wounded.
All is scarred. No longer
guaranteed forever sharp scared. Just scarred.
Scarred
Tainted

Haunted
Shellshocked
Out!
Every time you see a ram?

Oh god, when will we unbind?

16

Isaac, dear Isaac.
We deserved better.

Thirty years, three thousand years
and counting.

I wish us peace.
I wish us peace

unbridled, unbounded,
unthinkable peace

IV

Cut the Line and Live

Pink Impatiens

The woman in the pink house with pink impatiens
mowing her lawn in a pink shirt hasn't arrived,
hasn't heard her call, but fashions her relations
in the singular case, no case at all.
Better to realize
that the animals who grow most leap into their fears.
In high tide the rock crab likes to visualize
himself as a five-petaled flower, till he disappears
without himself and yet within; he rises and dives.
So with the nature of identity, it spins on
the axis of sacrifice while orbiting an unbroken sun.

In the second after the almost-accident,
for instance. Your hands burn: the provident
present yet so nearly absent that you dangle,
you waver; like clouds moving two ways
at the same time and passing each other,
you pass yourself, wonder at the story of your life, or rather
its near miss, and, if you really matter,
who are you? A silken tangle
of denial and desire, suspicion and faith,
disfigurement and beauty, mania and peacefulness.
Is this how God comes to us?

Numbers

Twenty-seven.
Twenty-seven years hijacked.
Twenty-seven thousand times
my hands are claws, clenched.
My right foot tries to brake
before I break.
Right foot brakes but I can't stop
what happened
twenty-seven years ago:
December seventeenth, a winter wedding.
Twenty-three years old.
Old enough to know or not?
Not, for I'd been raped at fifteen.
A girl, just.

At forty-two I realized I'd been raped
twenty-seven years earlier.
Too broken by rape to know that I'd been raped.
Too young to drive when raped.
I couldn't brake and so I broke.

Broken, then, at twenty-one.
Six years already hijacked by rape
when I met my second captor, actor superb.
I thought that I was safe.
December wedding: Did my foot try to brake?
For now it never stops.
I try to change time, change history.
I don't want that wedding,
those years, this life.
Twenty-seven thousand times
my right foot tries to brake
but I can't stop.

Broken for good.

Can't change   the numbers.
Can't unmeet   my captors.
Can't un-rape   my girlself.
Can't rewind   my wedding.

But can speak the truth.

Sanctuary 2

From whatever you leave behind

    A vase of blooming peonies
    on an altar once revered
    Broken bread and wine

From whatever it is you leave

        The beauty of cathedral
        A house worth half a million
        Your children's voices every day
        Your power to protect them

Look ahead, for these will move you forward

    Tiny lights in tree limbs
        The darkness of his lashes
            The slight curve of her cheek

   You are not alone

Leave behind the vase of peonies
    Leave the altar for your soul

Filled with Ladders, the World

*Contemporaneously created with Sofiya Inger's painting of
"The World is Filled with Ladders"*

My father's hands hold metal legs,
      I on the ladder's penultimate rung
  last-but-one-any-higher-too-high.
My father's hands hold metal legs,
    I scoop wet leaves from the rooftop gutter,
        first-house gutter, wet brown leaves,
    soft green moss. I pry the screen off, sharp,
        slide my fingers underneath, my fingers which,
  long ago held white string, Jacob's ladder.

Strong-girl hands with slender fingers hold
      Cat's Cradle, Jacob's ladder
    she climbs from seeds, from the singing bell
        the ringing bell, the bicycle bell
          the sweet-girl voice counts
        the ball and jacks singing
Jacob's ladder, fingering string and jacks
          and feet lift from the ground
to jump the rope to count to sing to lift
    past faces, past light, *the faces are the light*
      voices present voices past
rise past singing ringing fingers hands

Solid as stone the ground, light as flowers her feet
    ascend descend, spill through time like purple flowers

My father's hands hold metal stems
        and purple flowers spill through time
    we float through time on singing bells

    and ringing bells, the ball and jacks
      —the ball and chain pull us down
how dreadful is this place where tiny men would
   pull us down, we float up past
     my mother's face, your mother's voice
   the voices of our mothers
lift us sing us ring us past the sun and moon
   the stars at night *ascend descend and rise again*

The world is filled with my father's hands
   my mother's voice, the rungs of the crib
    your father's hands free you from
the rungs of your crib, we float we lift
    ascend through time, time present, time past
      —the ball and chain a nightmare dream
   as we float through the purple flowers
    the ball becomes *a singing bowl*
a ringing bell, the chain *a string a seed a stem*
     the ball and jacks, the jumping rope
the faces *stars* the faces *moons,* they lift me sing me
   ring me toward or ring me through
    the girlhood string of Jacob's ladder
  Jacob's gate, we float we rise
    through purple-flowered strings of time
how dreadful is that darkened place, those tiny men
    will never hold us down

My father's hands and mother's voice
     your mother's hands and father's voice
   my daughter's hands, my son's voice
  strong as stone and sweet as bells
  the singing voice, the ringing voice
the world is filled with voices past and voices now
    singing bells and ringing bells
     voices light leaves and bells

    suns and moons and purple flowers
Jacob's ladders fill the world, daughters sons
        stems and seeds, the world is filled with
    ladders made from faces light
and moss-rich earth   this place is filled with
      I dreamt it on stone   angels

No Matter

After Julie Eflin's watercolor "Looking Out, Looking In: Contemplating Who to Be"

No matter how I twist and turn,
no matter that you see me as granite,
   the x-ray shows flesh prickling, lips cool.
A survivor, I startle.

No longer a matter of no.
When injured, pieces fall like a disappearing language.
Left with neither present nor absent,
   I toss, I turn.

It remains, then, a matter of knowing,
   what to shed and what to keep.
Rose window, staircase, perception cloaked in sunlight.
No, night now tips the scale.
I drop shadows yet they find me,
I drop worry yet it finds me, fear and fury find me.

Shadows fall on darkness   fall on granite   fall on fury
   fall on flesh   fall on language   fall on flight
Hands capture light   capture shadow   capture darkness
   past the staircase   past the window   past my sight
Limbs index wounds   index worry   index darkness
   record fear   record sorrow   record night
Wrists cover eyes   cover judgment   cover darkness
   mask perception   mask invention   mask insight
Lips seek release   seek awareness   seek renewal
   release language   release silence   release

No matter hardship, flesh turns, despite shadow,
   despite darkness, flesh twists toward a matter of knowing.

A Simple Meal

Alone on the terrace with champagne,
the vesper sky. A single starling hops
on polished concrete. Two honeybees
circle then rise, dart low, then rise,
playful as my children. Broken heart inside,
not by a twenty-year lie,
broken by their absent eyes.

Silver lanterns warm evening air.
So much is lessened by the kindness of strangers.
Yet bereft, bereft of their citrus-scented skin!
I breathe, instead, the trail of a cigarette.
Nothing can satisfy this hunger.
A single scarlet poppy stretches toward a twilight sky;
pale yellow companions blow long-stemmed in the wind.

St. Helena, California

St. Helena, who are you?
Your vineyards and verdant hills,
your early-morning mist,
I've had my fill
of plucking and pruning,
branches left with nothing.
Too much taken, too much pruned.
Son's voice and daughter's voice,
these were not to go.

St. Helena, who are you?
Patron of the empty?
Vines crisscross my window,
sparrows won't be quiet.
The children's voices echo—
Indiana's far away,
I need to see them now.
Too much taken, too much pruned.
Shadows fall on dusty hills.

St. Helena. Who are you?
Flowers overflowing,
endless rows of ripened grapes.
The wind contains
my daughter's voice,
a mist-filled valley,
thoughts of son.
Saturday's too far away,
the beauty here, too much.

Eddie and Donald

Giggling girls have power the radio tells me
after the election. An epidemic of contagious

laughter spread through a girls' school
in Africa in 1962, and no one then knew why.

Hearing this carries a now-giggling
me back to my 5th grade classroom—to tiny

freckles on Eddie's nose, sprinkled sweet
as whispers. My girl-small hands unfold a scrap

of notebook paper, where penciled print
asks, *Do you like Eddie? Circle: Yes or No*

I circle *Yes*, for I like his tiny freckles and boy-sweet
smile, the sweep of his hair, dark across

brilliant blue eyes. Thin-boy Eddie, sweet-boy
Eddie, early love a tender age those tiny

freckles tic-tacked on that sweet-boy Ed—but
Tic Tacs startle me back to the radio's

blaring news, to the president-elect and
to trauma to groping assaulting abusing refuting

all that is tender and good in this world.
Oh, take me back to Eddie's sweet-breathed

boyhood face, those tiny freckles sprinkled light
and me nearby, carried away in giggling.

Simple Palms

1

The palm trees were beautiful.
This, I admit. But my trauma
came with me to the Florida Keys.

When gulls circled greedily
gullible beat through my brain.
When hermit crabs hid deep
in their shells, I asked to join.

The palm trees were beautiful
but they spoke of a certain Sunday,
waving and whispering memories:

One came to town on an ass's colt.
Another came in a Prius.
One was God. The other not.
Palm Sunday, the beginning of the end.

2

Palms. Psalms. Psalm 23.
Yea, though I walk through the valley
I will fear no—where were You?
I was never more alone.
The parched palms whisper
Palm Sunday. I arrived that day with
Husband. Pastor. Abuser.
Palm Sunday. The beginning. The end.

3

We moved to town in a Prius
and a Subaru. He drove
the Prius to look environmental.
Everything calculated.
Nothing loving. Nothing kind.
Just bruised arms and terror.

Palm branches flutter—if only
I could find a way to ease the pain.
Is it too much to ask for a quiet
way forward?
Can't palm trees simply be
beautiful in the breeze?

Whiplash

Red: the color of his face.
White: my knuckles as he threw
his cell phone, shattered
the windshield while driving.
Blue: the bruises he put on my forearms.
The personal and political merge,
pull me to the ground
    like gravity.
This is not normal, they say.
They call it whiplash, say it's why
we're all so tired: Twitter this
& Twitter that. I lived this insanity
for twenty-seven years. Thought
Trump's would end with the boast
that he can grab us by the—
    What am I
having for dinner? I ask, for all else
is too much, can't be stashed
in the nook of my grandmother's
desk, the secret nook my father used
as a child. Her desk became his
now it's mine. Someday it will belong
to my daughter or my son. The things
we inherit mark us: this desk, that clock,
that table. No. Not the table,
    too much history
there. I try again to stash but can't.
Rape simply can't be stashed.
Physical urticaria, the doctor tells me,
your skin cannot bear friction.
I can bear no friction. Trump's words
from *Access Hollywood* make me break

into a rash. I think, instead, of my
daughter's paintings, my son's
dark eyes, the fact that women have
the right to vote
    our president an abuser
Already reliving past trauma, now
I live this as well. *This and that,
that and this.* I spoon gelato
into my mouth, search for sweetness.
Simply not enough.

B-Side

What is to be done with this
overwhelming grief?
The courtyard, grief.
The valley, grief.
Years lost with my son, grief.
And yet the courtyard, the valley, my son.
This place is marked by the softness
of evening air and the kindness
of strangers. By endless grapes
on rolling hills. By vineyards flowing.
My son's moon-shaped face
so near, so light till I left his dad,
shattered the illusion.
Is there a B-side to grief?
Silhouettes of trees reach
toward the sky. Sunset blazes
behind lightless
hills, these hills larger at night,
the valleys darker. On this pitch-black
road, two rows of reflectors
flank a double solid line, then a single
row next to a broken
line. I drive, search. It's time
to cross the valley—but I can't find
a road. Sunset gone.
No moon yet.
I can't find a road.

Ghazal to Prey No More

Emily Doe, a Silence Breaker. Now Turner terms a trash bin prejudicial: says not to ignore
that he didn't hide his sexual assault behind a dumpster. His goal? Reputation restored.

Ashley Judd, Rose McGowan speak. Tarana Burke's #MeToo goes viral, via Alyssa Milano.
Jodi Kantor, Megan Twohey, Ronan Farrow write. Weinstein et al. can't deny anymore.

At CBS & NBC, NPR & Fox. In Congress Conyers & Kihuen. Farenthold, Franken
& Franks. Assaulters & harassers. Rapists & child molesters. Named like never before.

No Eleventh Commandment: Thou shalt not prey on teenage girls. So he hides behind
the Bible. But mall, loopy scrawl on a card & a yearbook—Truth did out, judge Moore.

Never was challenged: Moved up judicial ranks on false pretense of being a fair, wise man.
But Kavanaugh displayed hypocrisy and rage, thanks to the courage of Christine Blasey Ford.

"I moved on her like a bitch . . . You can do anything. Grab 'em by the pussy." Trump denies,
but a tape says otherwise. Summer Zervos sues. Will he grope again? Let's pray no more.

Time to speak: Me too. My husband raped me. A pastor, in public hid
 behind his collar.
In private called choir girls "hot," watched porn, forced me to do what he
 knew I abhorred.

How many silent survivors? Hotel housekeepers, lobbyists, fruit pickers,
 college students,
etc., etc. What we say re: Trump, my ex-husband, et al.? Enough. The End.
 Never more.

Asleep, Awake, a Dream

Hope is a waking dream.
~ Aristotle

1. Nightmare

In the passenger seat I, more fragile
than a snowdrop, had to promise
I wouldn't be myself, or else
he wouldn't drive me home.
Route 37, Cleveland,
Cuyahoga's pewter sky.

too many memories, another life

Swisshotel Chicago:
"Shut. Up." he snarled.
"How dare you want the light off?"
I'm smaller than a snowdrop.

2. Dream

In my dream I spill coffee and
the car careens off the road uphill,
casts tire tracks on tender soil.

I get out. No way home.
Lost in the station, can't read the map.
Fire alarm, flashing lights
—*urgent message when flashing*—
Evacuate the station

Wait, a train arrives, a woman helps me on.
Two young women count out my coins.
The driver interrupts, "Phone call for you."
A train's corded phone.
I grasp the plastic handle, place it to my ear:
"You. Are. Fired." *You don't exist.*
You'll never make it home.

"She'll go back to him," my friend said.
But I didn't.

3. Hijacked

Granville beckons. Or Grandview?
Wherever I got the ticket.
The payphone where I cried.
Leaving you two behind was
never going to work.

Scripted food for his ego:
How dare you want the light off!
How dare you want to sleep!
    to sleep, to rest, to be . . .
The TV's lurid color flashes past my eyes
—*urgent message when flashing*—

Empty. Nothing.
Hijacked. So many years hijacked.

My dream for you, daughter—my dream
for daughter and son—always remember:
I left the payphone, not you.

Hijacked by fear, by terror.
Stayed another fifteen years *the age when I was raped:*

a girl, doe-like, like you, daughter,
but three years younger.
A future hijacked.

The first time I was raped
—*urgent message when flashing*—

The clematis spills off the fence onto grass onto patio,
covering weeds and hiding cracked concrete.

4. Ohio, Awake

My daughter beside me,
I try to go back to sleep
but my whole body aches from
arthritis, hotel bed, Ohio.

Daughter, you were made by an exploding star,
its iron in your blood.
We were made by an exploding star,
with iron in our blood.

When you visit your godparents, far from his reach,
my worry is gone. Simply gone.

5. Dream

Asleep. Awake. A dream.
Dogwood petals flutter, wind chimes ring,
tiny yellow-finch bodies pepper the air
    a self in small form

The dogwood petals fall to earth, but this
is summer, not spring. Spring, not summer.

Blossoms fall in spring. Or autumn. Fall.
I fall. I wake.
    never hit ground in a dream
The radio's drone drowns out the darkness.

We came with dreams. Dream, I said,
for it keeps the world spinning.
But the world wasn't spinning, just me.

My dream for you, daughter,
my dream for you, son,

my dreams asleep,
the Sandman's hands gently stir them
keeping them alive.
My dreams alive,
for I am dead.

I was dead
    smaller than a snowdrop
    more fragile than a snowdrop
One o'clock and the house is cold,
the windows clear but nothing inside.

The children washed the windows,
all twenty-two, while I was on retreat.
And he fumed. No food for his ego.

I couldn't walk the labyrinth.
The dream gone. Never alive, in fact.
You shattered the illusion,
my son's butterfly face whispered to me.

The sound of the stars, like crickets.
What do we hold onto?

A dreamer, I am, and the world is still spinning.
Step off and find, what?

My dream for her, for him, for me

Why did I hold onto nothing?
I was holding onto nothing.

No. *I held your faces, stars, the iron of your blood
exploding, always, in mine.*

His First Wife

> *and victory filled up*
> *the little rented boat . . .*
>
> ~ Elizabeth Bishop, "The Fish"

He'd caught her
like a fish.
That's how
he told it
when asked
how they met.
"I had to
get it right
just once," he'd say.
"I got it
right with
my first wife."
As he spoke
he would
demonstrate
precisely
how he'd played
the catch:

Right hand flung
behind right shoulder
left hand
in front of his face
as he tipped back
and cast
the make-believe line
which had

perfectly
snagged her.

Next, right hand
drew quick
small circles and
both hands glided
toward his jaw
as he reeled her in
deliberately.

She listened
to his story
and wondered
(as they were
still married)
at his use of
the phrase
first wife
though he said it
always
with a chuckle.

One day
his words
formed a hook
in her mouth.
She tasted blood.

So she
cut the line
and lived.

www.ingramcontent.com/pod-product-compliance
Lightning Source LLC
Chambersburg PA
CBHW070258100426
42743CB00011B/2255